DATA HANDLING

ACTIVITY BOOK FOR CHILDREN

Count and tally.

Count and color the graph accordingly.

	6				
	5				
	4				
	3				
	2				
	1				

Wonder House

Bar Graph

A bar graph is a visual representation of data using horizontal and rectangular bars of different lengths. It helps to show and compare quantities or values in a simple and easy-to-understand manner. Bar graphs encourage critical thinking and foster deeper understanding of data handling through visual representation.

The image below shows the different types of fishes in an aquarium. Explore the kid-friendly bar graph. Count and color the bars to represent the quantity of each fish.

a) Color the bar graph.

b) Which fish appears the most and which fish appears the least?

....

c) How many fishes are there in the aquarium?

....

Pie Chart

A pie chart is a circular visual representation of data. It is divided into proportional slices depicting quantities or different categories.

In a survey about marine life preferences among kids, crabs emerged as the kids' favorite. Starfish, jellyfish, and whales followed in descending order. Color the slice with the crab red, whale blue, jellyfish pink and starfish green.

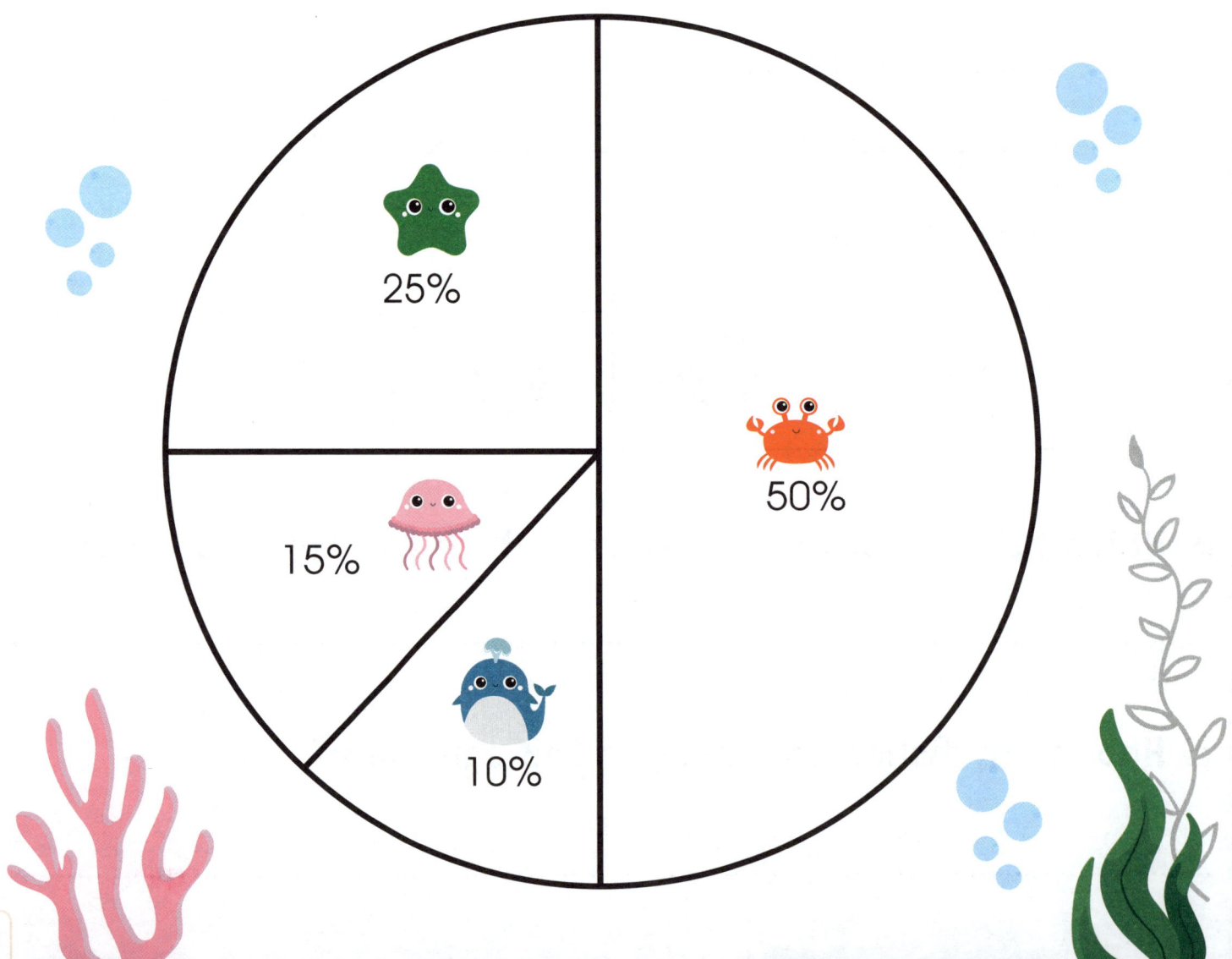

a) Which is the least popular marine animal?

....

b) What is the percentage of the least favorite marine animal?

....

c) What percentage of kids like starfish and jellyfish?

....

d) What is another way of saying 50%?

....

e) Name two other marine animals that you know of.

....

Tally

A tally for kids is a simple counting system using vertical lines to represent numbers. Each fifth line is crossed, making it easy to track and display quantities in a visual way.

How many ladybugs and snails do you see? Use tally marks to record your observations in the space given below.

a)

b)

c)

Given below are some Dinos waiting to be rescued. Count the number of dinosaurs and prepare the Tally chart.

a)

b)

c)

d)

Pictograph

Color the different shapes given in the ball. Then, complete the graph by counting the number of each shape and coloring the graph accordingly. Answer the questions that follow.

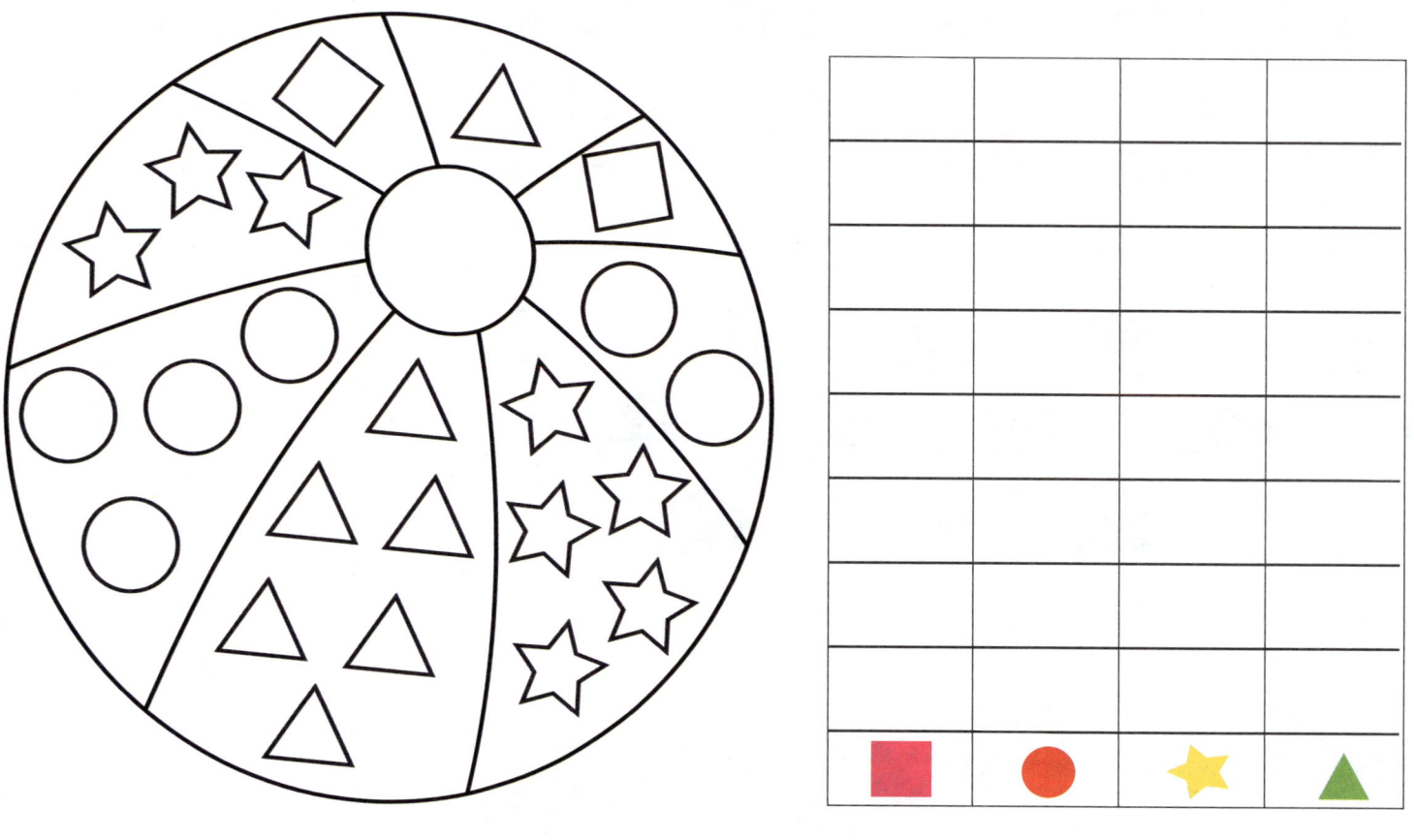

a) Which shape has the highest count?

....

b) Which shape has the lowest count?

....

Let's Tally!

Look at this pictograph carefully. Count the number of objects you can see and prepare a Tally chart in the given space.

a)

b)

c)

Favorite Day of the Week

The teacher in a classroom of **40** students asked them what day of the week is their favorite. She called out the days of the week and the kids raised their hands. Answer a few questions on the basis of the bar graph given below–

a) Monday is the favorite day of how many children?

....

b) How many students like the Weekend (including both Saturday and Sunday)?

....

c) How many days are there in a week?

....

d) Which is the most favorite day of the students during the week?

....

e) Which is the least favorite day of the students during the week?

....

f) Do you like the weekend? What do you like to do on your day off?

....

Snoopy's Candies

Snoopy loves candies and he got a bagful of his favorite candies this Halloween! The following graph shows how much candy Snoopy ate in the month of November. Answer the following questions after studying the pie chart carefully.

	M&M's		Reese's Cups		Toblerone		KitKat
	Skittles		Jolly Rancher		Hershey's Chocolate Bars		

a) What all chocolates did Snoopy eat during the month of November?

....

....

b) Which chocolate did Snoopy enjoy eating the most?

....

....

c) Which chocolate did Snoopy eat the least?

....

....

d) Which among these are the most colorful candies? Name at least two.

....

....

e) Write the names of all the candies you got in your last Trick or Treat.

....

....

Geometric Shapes

Look at the picture given below carefully and answer the questions given on Page 15. Color the picture using your favorite colors.

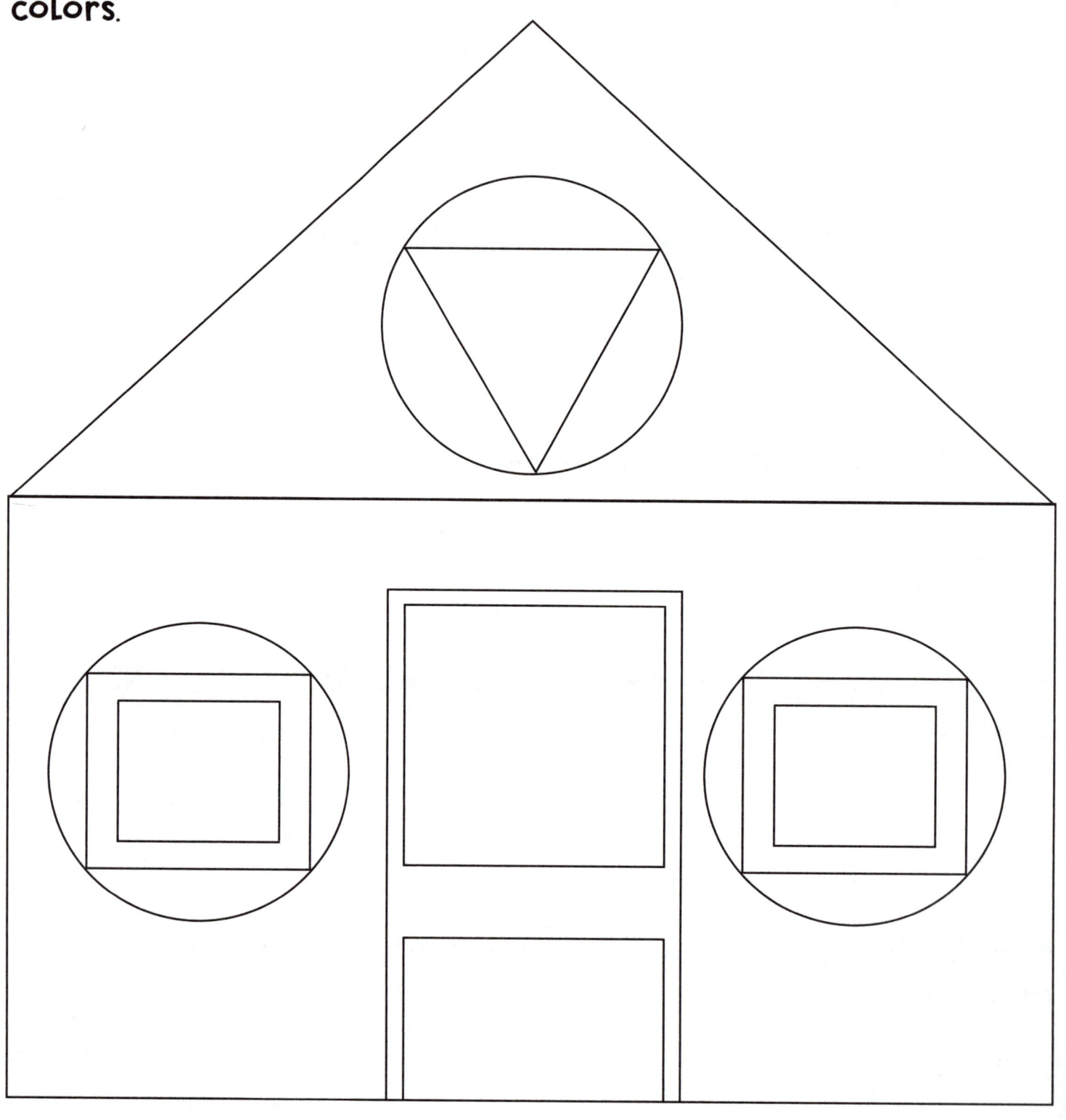

a) Name all the shapes that you can spot in this picture.

....

....

b) How many squares and rectangles can you spot in the picture?

....

....

c) Count the number of shapes you can see in the picture.

....

....

d) Name and draw the shape that occurs the least number of times in the picture.

Ice Cream Flavors

A survey was conducted in a classroom with 30 students about their favorite Ice Cream flavor. Following is a pictograph representing the choices each student made.

S.No.	Ice Cream Flavor	Number of Students
1	Chocolate	😊 😊 😊 😊 😊 😊
2	Vanilla	😊 😊 😊 😊 😊
3	Cookies and Cream	😊 😊 😊 😊 😊 😊 😊
4	Strawberry	😊 😊 😊 😊
5	Mint Chocolate Chip	😊 😊 😊 😊 😊
6	Butterscotch	😊 😊 😊

Each 😊 represents 1 student in the class.

a) How many students like Chocolate and Mint Chocolate Chip Flavor?

....

b) How many students like Cookies and Cream?

....

c) Which flavor is most and least liked by the students?

....

d) Which flavors are chunky in texture?

....

e) Draw a picture of your favorite ice cream in the given space.

Marble Trouble

Sheena had **4** marbles in her bag, while Ronan had **9** in his. Shane had only **2**. Answer the questions based on the given information–

a) How many marbles do the three of them have in total?

....

b) Who has the most number of marbles?

....

c) Who has the least number of marbles?

....

d) How many marbles will Sheena, Ronan and Shane have in total, if Snoopy gives them 5 of his marbles?

....

e) How many marbles will be left if Snoopy takes away Sheena's marbles?

....

Sort and Tally

Given below are some everyday objects. Sort and categorize the objects based on their shapes and prepare a tally chart.

Shapes	Number of Objects
Rectangle	
Circle	
Semi circle	
Crescent	
Octagon	

Summer Fruits

Given below is a list of some Summer fruits. Count the number of letters that each fruit has and write them in the given space.

S T R A W B E R R Y

C H E R R I E S

W A T E R M E L O N

A P P L E

M A N G O

P I N E A P P L E

B A N A N A

A V O C A D O

a) How many fruits have 5 Letters?

....

b) How many times does the Letter R appear in the names of all fruits?

....

c) How many times does the Letter A appear in the names of all fruits?

....

d) Data for how many Summer fruits is given?

....

e) Name the fruits which are bigger in size.

....

f) Name the fruits that are yellow and orange in color.

....

g) Which is your favorite fruit among these?

....

Katy's Boutique

Katy has a boutique with trendy outfits. This is a pictograph that shows what garments were sold to the customers in a week. Study it carefully and answer the questions.

S.No.	Garment	Number of Customers
1	Skirts	🛍️🛍️🛍️🛍️🛍️
2	Polo T-shirts	🛍️🛍️🛍️🛍️
3	Denim Jeans	🛍️🛍️🛍️🛍️🛍️🛍️
4	Denim Jackets	🛍️🛍️🛍️🛍️🛍️🛍️🛍️
5	Leggings	🛍️🛍️🛍️

Each 🛍️ represents 5 customers at the boutique.

a) How many customers bought Denim Jackets?

....

b) How many T-shirts were sold during one week?

....

c) What were the total number of garments sold during the week?

....

d) Which garment was sold the least and the most?

....

e) What would you wear among these to a party with your friends? Draw and color your outfit in the space below.

Musical Survey

At a recently held Music Festival, a survey on "Preferred Music Genre" was conducted with some people attending the festival. Given below is a graph documenting the responses. Study it carefully before answering the questions that follow.

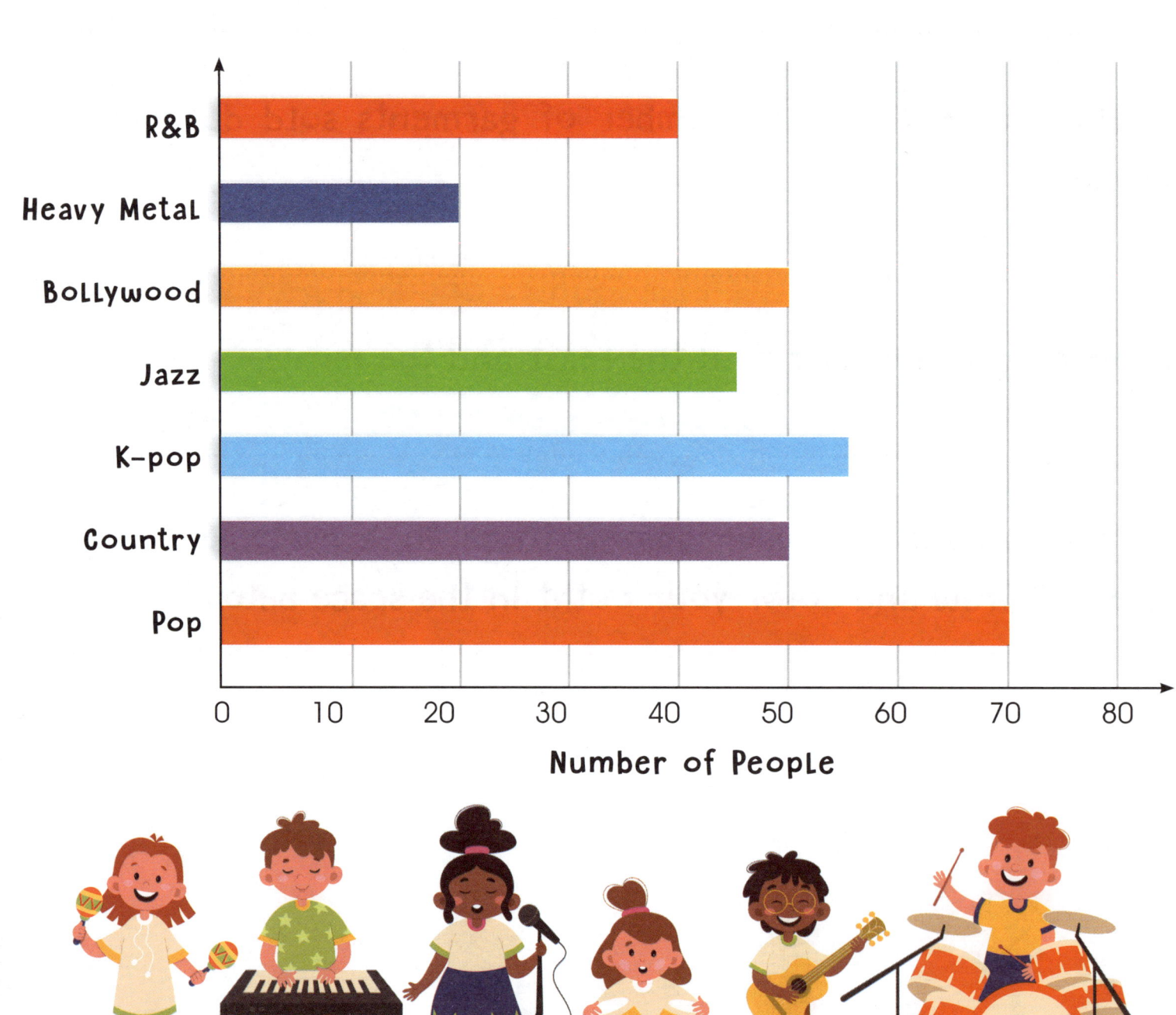

a) Which genre of music is most popular amongst the people?

....

b) How many people like Jazz music?

....

c) Which is the least popular genre of music?

....

d) How many people listen to Country and K-pop music?

....

e) Trace the dots on these music instruments and fill colors.

Modes of Transport

Given below is a Tally chart that shows the number of people who travel to school by different modes of transport. Answer the following questions based on the given information:

Mode of Transport		Number of People
	Car	⌗⌗ ⌗⌗ |||
	Bus	⌗⌗ ⌗⌗ ⌗⌗ ||||
	Bicycle	⌗⌗ ||

a) What is the most used mode of transport?

....

b) How many students go by bus?

....

c) What is the Least used mode of transport?

....

d) How many students do not use bicycles?

....

Cookie Trouble

In a box of cookies, each cookie is supposed to have **4** chocolate chips. However, some cookies do not have the right amount of choco chips. Help Mimi find out how many cookies are defective by answering the following questions.

a) How many cookies in the box have the right number of choco chips?

....

b) How many cookies have only 3 choco chips?

....

c) What is the least number of choco chips in a cookie among these?

....

d) How many cookies are in one box?

....

Vegetable Farming

A farmer who has a large piece of land, cultivates 5 vegetables during the year. Study the pictograph and answer the following questions.

S.No.	Vegetables	Produce
1	Lettuce	🧺🧺
2	Cucumber	🧺🧺🧺🧺
3	Tomato	🧺🧺🧺🧺🧺🧺🧺🧺
4	Radish	🧺🧺🧺🧺🧺🧺
5	Carrot	🧺🧺🧺🧺🧺🧺🧺

Each 🧺 represents 10kg of the produce.

a) What quantity of Tomatoes does the farmer produce?

....

b) Which is the most produced vegetable during the year?

....

c) What is the quantity of the Least produced vegetable?

....

d) How many Kgs of Cucumber does the farmer produce?

....

e) The produce of Radish is Lesser to the produce of Carrot by

....

f) The produce of Cucumber is Lesser to the produce of Radish by

....

Visitors at the Zoo

Little children love to visit the Zoo with their parents. Given below is a bar graph showing how many Adults and Children visited the local Zoo, over a period of four months.

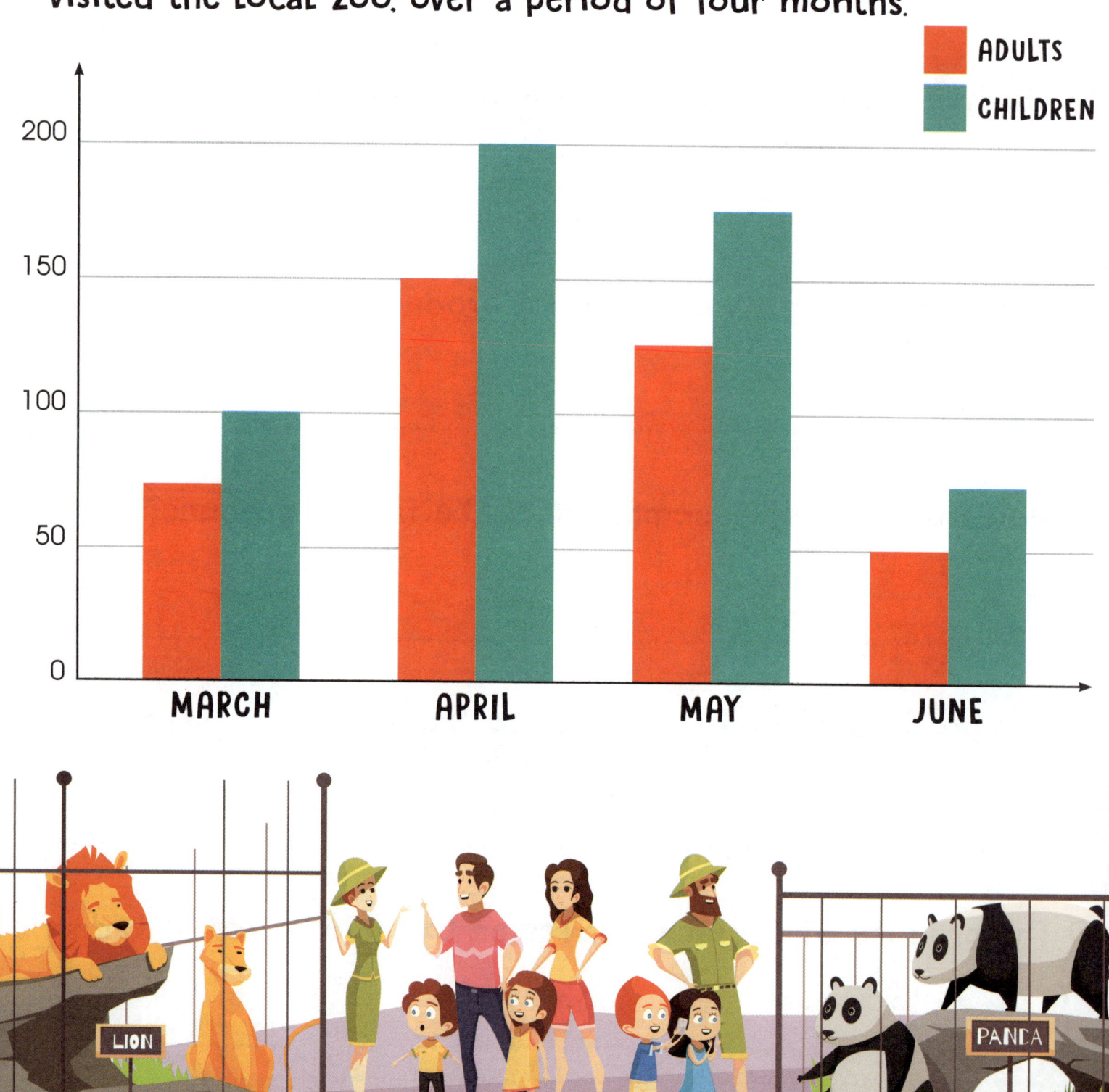

a) Which month saw the Least number of adults?

....

b) In which month did most adults visit the zoo?

....

c) What is the total number of children who visited the zoo during these four months?

....

d) How many Less adults compared to the children, went to the zoo during the month of May?

....

e) Have you ever visited your Local zoo? Name any 5 animals you saw at the zoo.

....

Shape Quest

Study the picture given below carefully. Now color the boxes as many times you can spot the shapes in the picture.

a) Name at least 3 shapes that can be seen in the given picture.

....

b) How many triangles can you spot in the picture?

....

c) What all shapes have been used to make the tree?

....

d) Which is the most used shape?

....

e) What are the shapes used in the picture called? Write in the space given below:

....

....

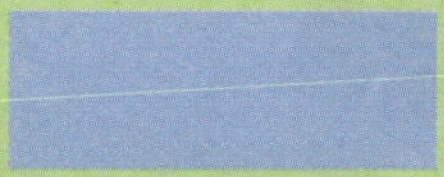

Sports Day

For the upcoming Annual Sports Day celebrations, a survey was conducted with members of a sports club. The following pie chart shows the number of people who are interested in playing different sports.

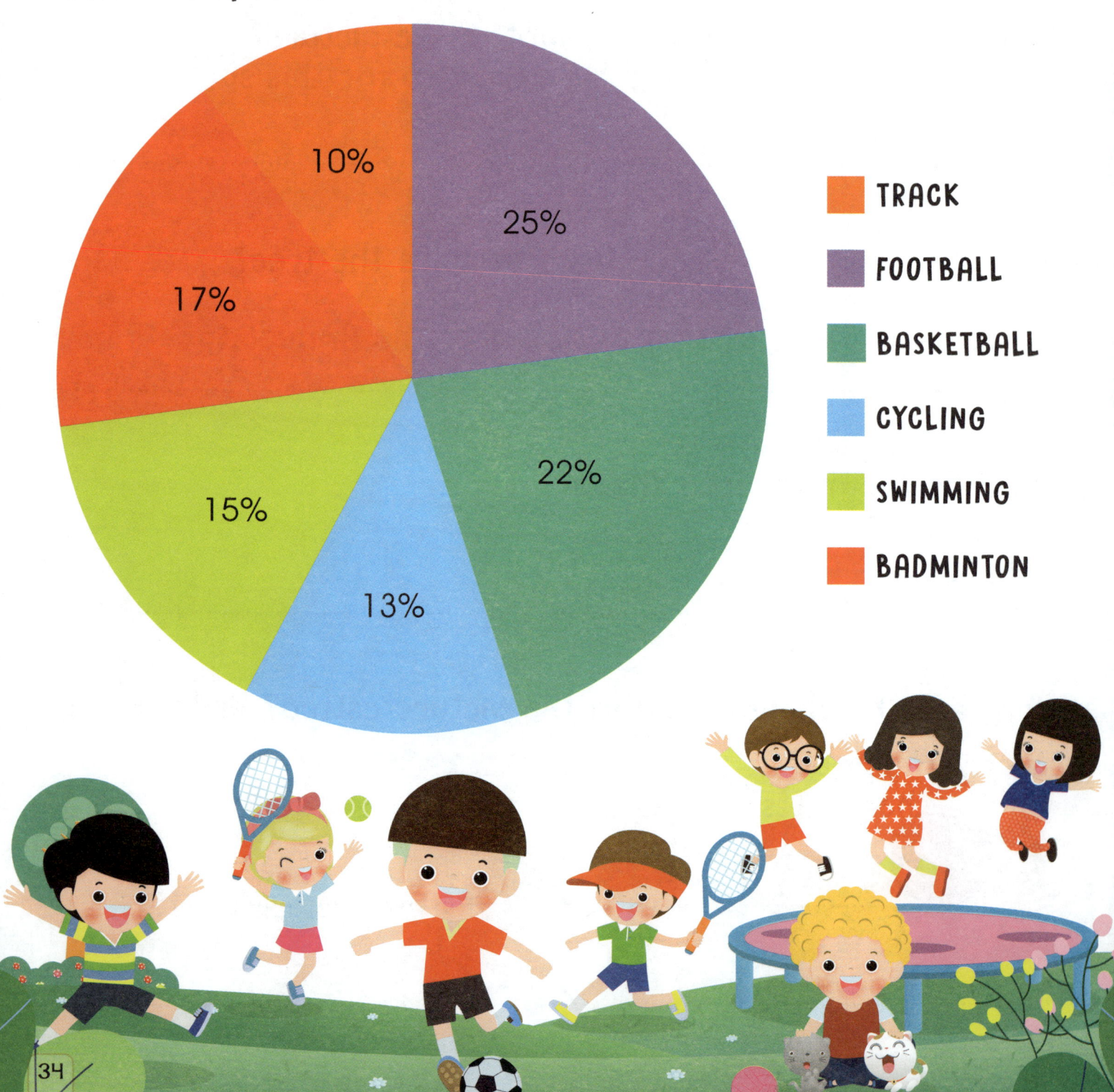

- TRACK
- FOOTBALL
- BASKETBALL
- CYCLING
- SWIMMING
- BADMINTON

a) Most of the club members signed up for this sport. Which sport is it?

....

b) Least number of the members signed up for this sport. Which sport is it?

....

c) What all sports are being featured in the Annual Sports Day celebrations?

....

....

d) Among the sports being played, which are required to use a ball?

....

Monthly Savings

My friends and I collect our savings all month long, and then have a party at the end of every month. The graph given below shows our monthly savings.

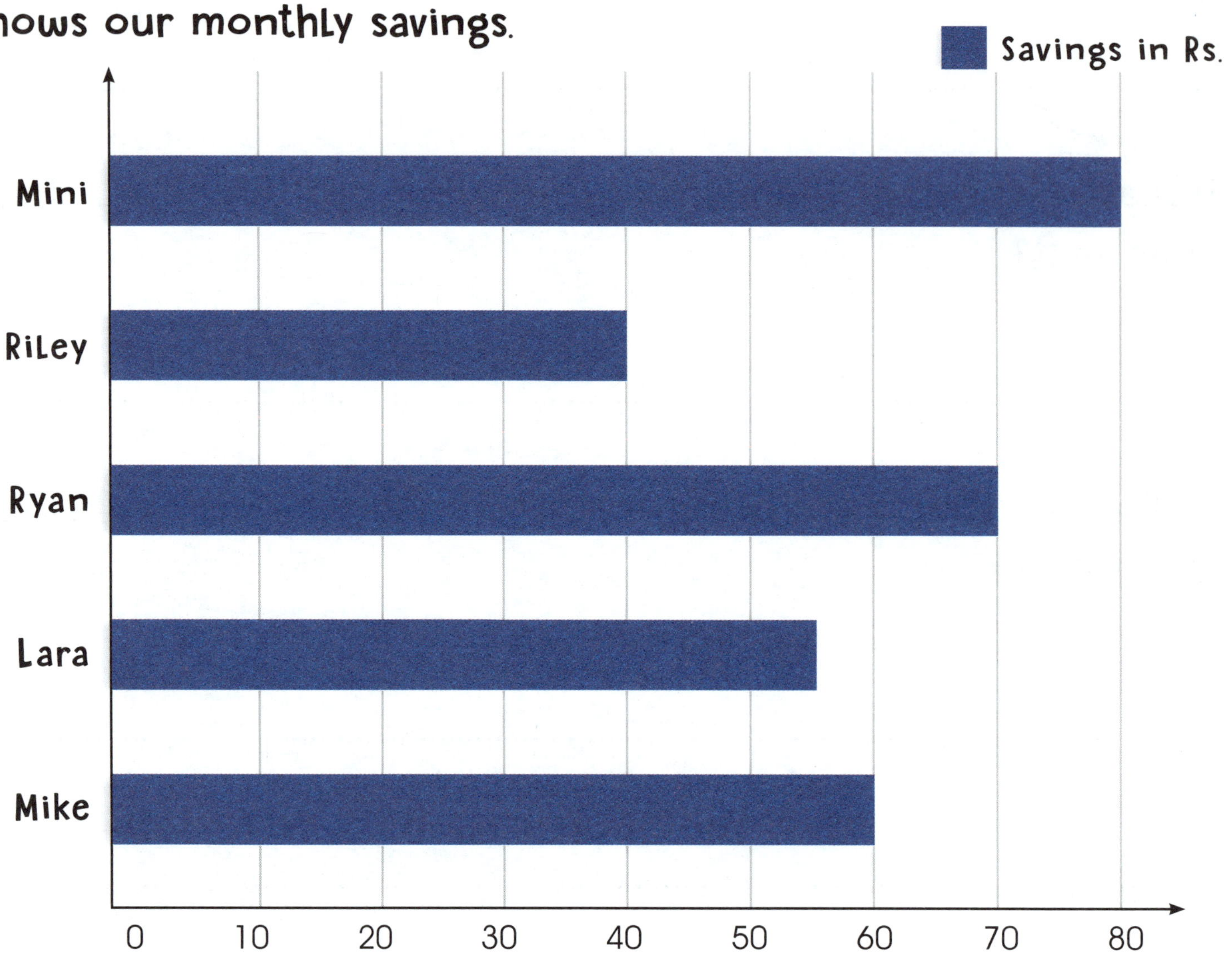

■ Savings in Rs.

Name	Savings (Rs.)
Mini	80
Riley	40
Ryan	70
Lara	55
Mike	60

a) How much money have the girls managed to save?

....

b) How much money have the boys saved in total?

....

c) By how much were Riley's savings less than Ryan's?

....

d) How much more did Mini save than Mike?

....

e) How much pocket money do you get every month?

....

f) How much money do you manage to save every month?

....

Student Enrollment Data

The given table shows the number of students enrolled in a school over a period of 4 years. Study the table carefully and answer the questions that follow.

Students	Year 2020	Year 2021	Year 2022	Year 2023
Girls	1300	1250	1700	2200
Boys	1650	2000	2150	2500

a) How many girl students were enrolled during the years 2021 and 2022?

....

b) How many boys have enrolled in the school in the last 4 years?

....

c) When was the number of girls lowest and highest among all the years?

....

d) When was the number of boys highest among all the years?

....

e) How many girl students were enrolled during the years 2022 and 2023?

....

f) Refer to the question on page 30 and try to visually depict the given information in the form of a bar graph, in the space given below.

Group Trip

A group of 50 people were asked if they were going on a trip. This bar graph given below shows their responses. Answer the questions that follow, based on the graph.

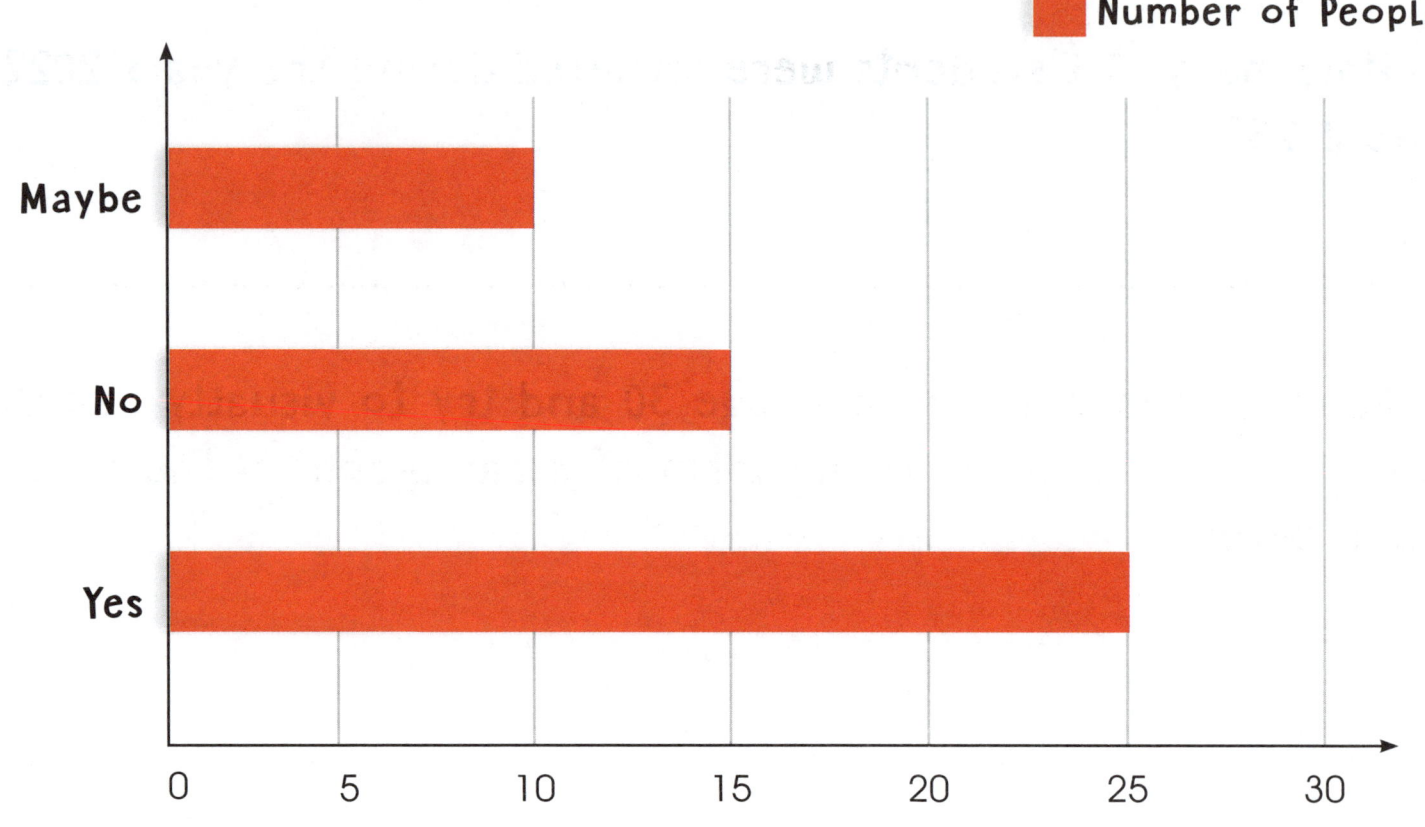

a) How many people are going on the trip?

....

b) How many people said they may or may not go on the trip?

....

c) How many people are not going on the trip?

....

d) Now, plan a family trip to a destination of your choice. Collect the data by asking all your family members if they want to go or not and accordingly record their responses. On the basis of the previous question, fill in the empty graph given below:

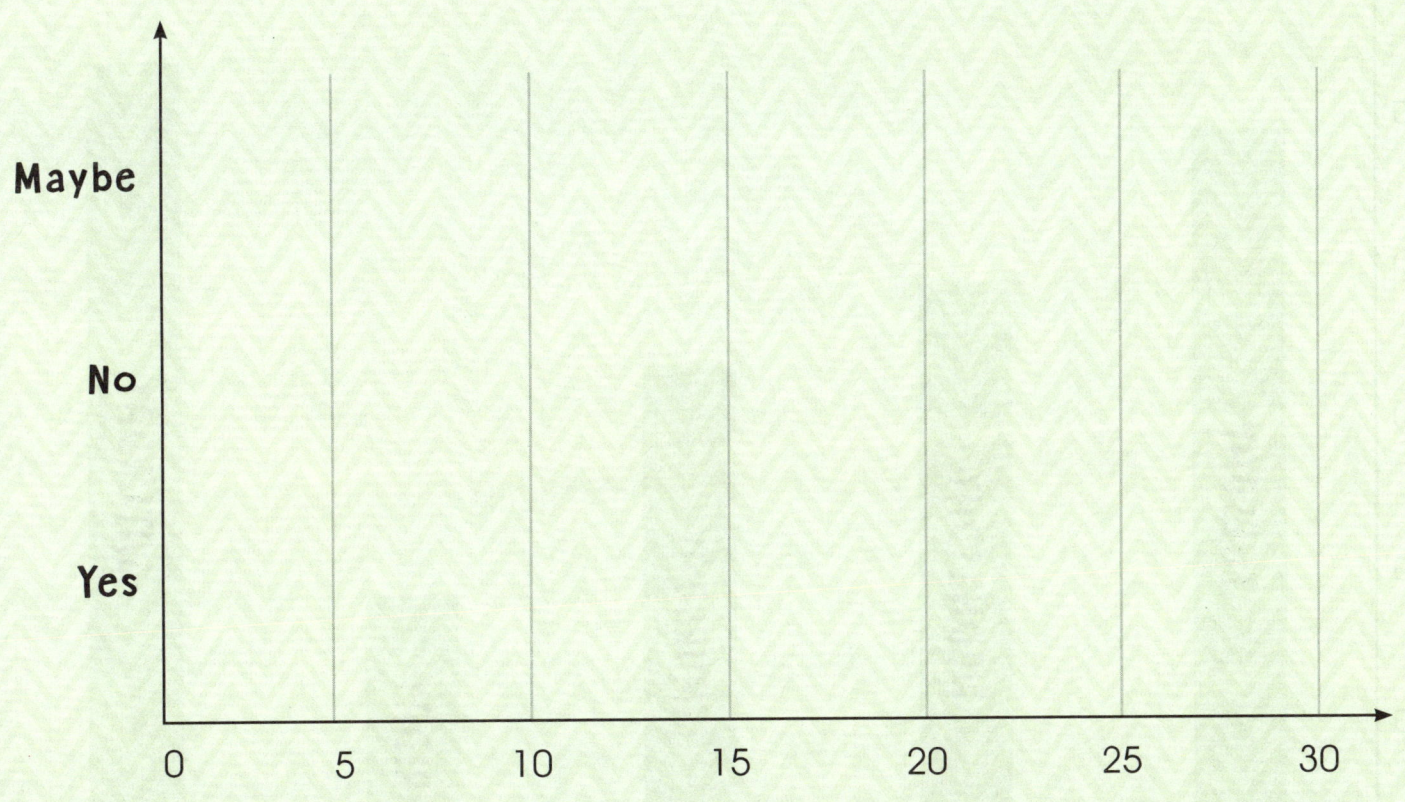

Visit to the Museum

The bar graph given below shows the number of visitors who visited the Art museum on 5 consecutive days in the month of August. Study the graph carefully and answer the questions.

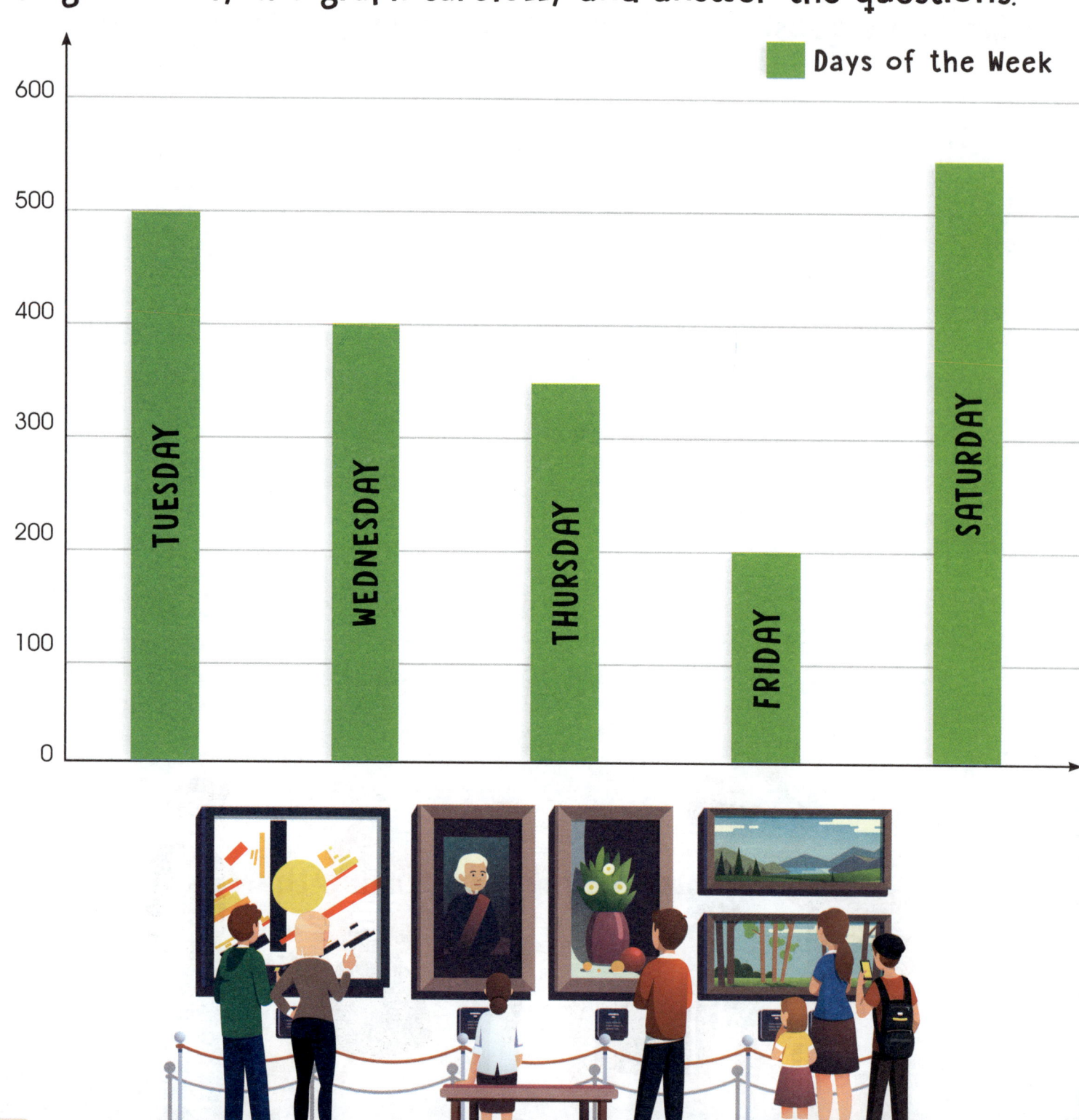

a) On which day 200 more people visited than Thursday?

....

b) What was the number of total visitors on Thursday, Friday and Saturday?

....

c) How many less visitors visited on Friday than Saturday?

....

d) What is the least number of people who visited during the week?

....

e) How many less people visited on Saturday than Tuesday and Wednesday combined?

....

Cars over the Years

The below graph shows the data of the sales recorded by big car brands during the years 2021, 2022 and 2023. Study the graph carefully and answer the following questions.

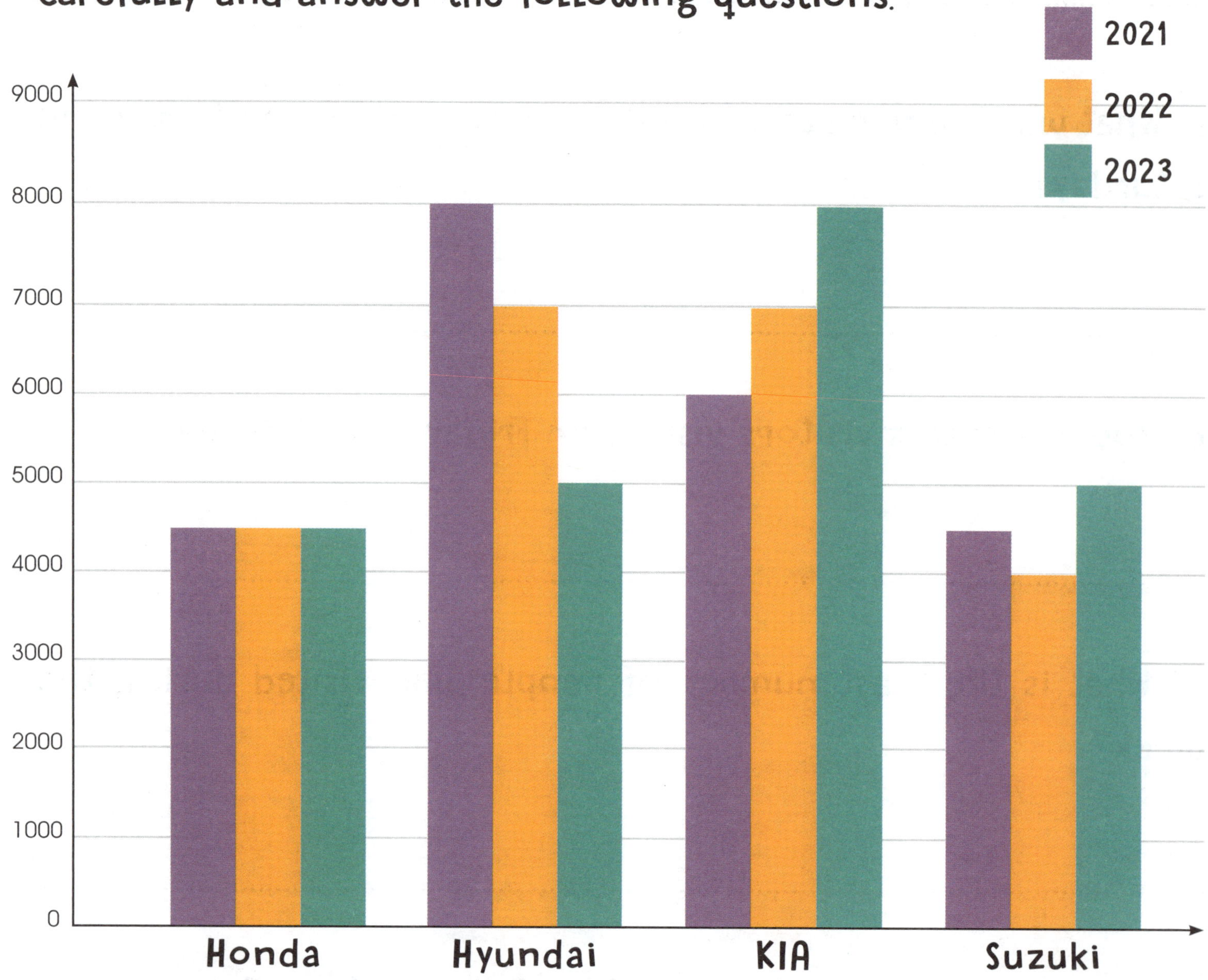

* The names of companies mentioned in this question are used for illustrative purposes only and are not part of any original statistical data.

a) The sales of which brand saw a steady decline during the survey period?

....

b) The sales of which brand saw a steady increase during 2021 to 2023?

....

c) The sales of which brand remained steady throughout the survey period?

....

d) Calculate the total number of sales for KIA during the 3 years.

....

e) By how much are the total sales of Suzuki less than the total sales of KIA?

....

Swimming Club

5 year old Jenny loves to swim. She has recently joined a swimming club. Here is the data of all the people who have enrolled in the Swimming club over the last three years.

Students	Year 2021	Year 2022	Year 2023
Girls	125	300	580
Boys	200	450	400
Men	350	520	640
Women	55	70	120

a) A total of how many people have enrolled in the Swimming Club during 2022?

....

b) When was the popularity of swimming the lowest, based on the statistics given?

....

c) How many women have signed up in total, during the last three years?

....

Answers

Page 3
a) Yellow fish: 7
Green fish: 6
Red fish: 7
Pink fish: 8,
b) Green fish,
c) 28

Page 5
a) Whale,
b) 10%,
c) 40%,
d) Half

Page 6
b) 卌 II,
c) 卌 IIII

Page 7
a) 卌 卌
b) 卌 卌 II
c) 卌 IIII
d) 卌 卌 II

Page 8
a) Star,
b) Square

Page 9
a) 卌 II,
b) 卌 IIII,
c) 卌 卌 III

Page 11
a) 10,
b) 22,
c) 7,
d) Sunday,
e) Tuesday

Page 13
a) M&M's, Reese's Cups, Toblerone, KitKat, Skittles, Jolly Rancher, Hershey's Chocolate Bars

Page 13
b) Skittles,
c) Jolly Rancher,
d) Skittles and M&M's

Page 15
a) Triangle
Circle
Square
Rectangle,
b) 5 squares and 3 rectangles,

Page 15
c) Square: 5
Rectangle: 3
Circle: 3
Triangle: 2

Page 17
a) 11, b) 7,
c) Cookies and Cream and buttersotch,
d) Cookies and cream, mint chocolate chip, butterscotch

Page 18
a) 15,
b) Ronan,
c) Shane,
d) 20 (15+5),
e) 11(15-4)

Page 19
a) Rectangle   卌,
b) Circle   I,
c) Semi-circle   卌,
d) Crescent   IIII,
e) Polygon   IIII

Page 20
10, 8, 10, 5, 5, 9, 6, 7

Page 21
a) 2, b) 6, c) 10,
d) 8,
e) Watermelon, pineapple,
f) Mango, pineapple, banana

Page 23
a) 35,
b) 20,
c) 125 garments,
d) Leggings and Denim jackets

Page 25
a) Pop,
b) 45,
c) Heavy Metal,
d) 105

Page 26
a) Bus,
b) 19,
c) Bicycle,
d) 32

Page 27
a) 1,
b) 3,
c) 2,
d) 6

Page 29	Page 31	Page 33	Page 35
a) 80 kg, b) Tomato, c) 20 kg, d) 40 kg, e) 10 kg, f) 20 kg	a) June, b) April, c) 550, d) 50	a) Circle, square, triangle, b) 4, c) Triangle and square, d) Circle, e) Circle, Square, Triangle, Rectangle	a) Football, b) Track, c) Track, football, basketball, swimming, cycling, badminton, d) Football and basketball

Page 37	Page 38	Page 40	Page 43
a) Rs. 135, b) Rs. 170, c) Rs. 30, d) Rs. 20	a) 2950, b) 8300, c) Lowest: 2021 Highest: 2023, d) 2023, e) 3900	a) 25, b) 10, c) 15	a) Saturday, b) 1100, c) 350, d) 200, e) 350

Page 45	Page 46
a) Hyundai, b) KIA, c) Honda, d) 21000, e) 7500	a) 1340, b) Year 2021, c) 245

Titles in the series

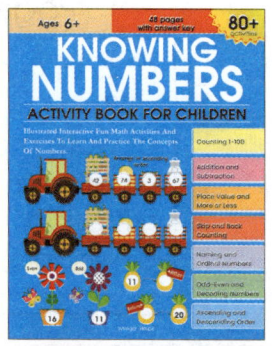

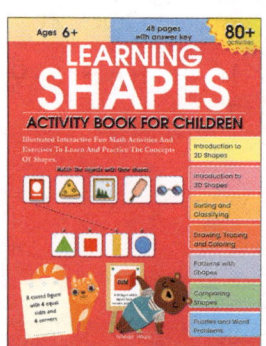

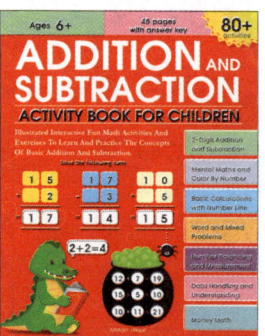

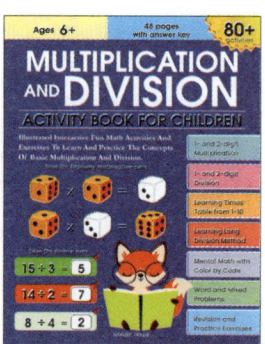

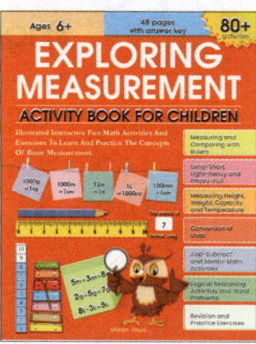

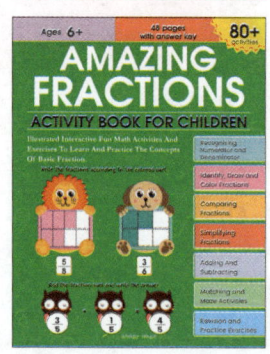

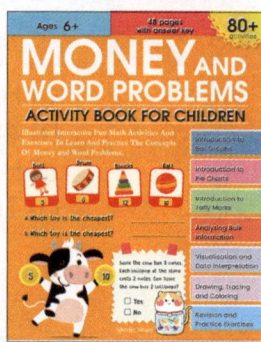